WORK

toward

REWARD

WORK
toward
REWARD

Building Business Value Today for a
Well-Deserved Future

Chia-Li Chien

iUniverse, Inc.
Bloomington

Work toward Reward
Building Business Value Today for a Well-Deserved Future

Copyright © 2012 by Chien Associates LLC.

All rights reserved. No part of this book may be used or reproduced by any means, graphic, electronic, or mechanical, including photocopying, recording, taping or by any information storage retrieval system without the written permission of the publisher except in the case of brief quotations embodied in critical articles and reviews.

iUniverse books may be ordered through booksellers or by contacting:

iUniverse
1663 Liberty Drive
Bloomington, IN 47403
www.iuniverse.com
1-800-Authors (1-800-288-4677)

Because of the dynamic nature of the Internet, any web addresses or links contained in this book may have changed since publication and may no longer be valid. The views expressed in this work are solely those of the author and do not necessarily reflect the views of the publisher, and the publisher hereby disclaims any responsibility for them.

Stories presented in this document are based on real clients and real situations. The names and facts in each case study have been changed to protect the privacy of the individuals or clients involved. However, use of business and individual names appearing in previously published articles and content were approved for these and other publication purposes.

This document is designed to provide readers with accurate and authoritative information regarding the subject matter covered. It is sold with the understanding that neither the author or her exit strategy consulting firm, Chien Associates LLC DBA Value Growth Institute, are engaged by the reader to provide or render legal, accounting or other professional advice. If legal, tax or other expert advice is sought or required by the reader, the services of competent professionals licensed to perform those services should be retained. The purpose of this document is to educate readers. The author and Chien Associates LLC DBA Value Growth Institute shall not have any liability or responsibility to any person or entity with respect to any loss or damage caused, or alleged to be caused, directly or indirectly by reliance on information contained in this book. If you do not wish to be bound by the above, you may return this document.

ISBN: 978-1-4759-4903-2 (sc)
ISBN: 978-1-4759-4905-6 (hc)
ISBN: 978-1-4759-4904-9 (ebk)

Library of Congress Control Number: 2012917097

Printed in the United States of America

iUniverse rev. date: 09/20/2012

Contents

Acknowledgements ix

The Research xi

Business Value Drivers Study xi

What Makes the BVD Study Valuable to You? xv

Chapter 1: Risk vs. Reward 1

Chapter 2: What impacts business value from an investor
   or buyer perspective? 4

Chapter 3: BVD study Mission Critical Activities 8

Chapter 4: Selected Interviews from the BVD Study 16

Chapter 5: BVD Study Conclusion 47

Appendix 1: BVD Study Results 53

Appendix 2: About The Study Participants 60

Appendix 3: Demographics of the participants 63

Appendix 4: How The Study Is Conducted 65

Appendix 5: How The Interview Is Conducted 68

Appendix 6: Transfer Methods 71

Bibliography 81

About Chia-Li Chien 85

Other Books by Chia-Li Chien 87

Index 89

Dedicated to:

my parents,

my husband TC and

my daughter Con-Ning.

Thank you for giving me much pride and support.

Acknowledgements

Special thanks to Tension Management Institute for providing ChangeGrid and its methods to facilitate this study.

T. Falcon Napier

Tension Management Institute

http://www.tensionmanagementinstitute.org

Thank you to all participants who took time to complete the assessments and interview.

The Research

Business Value Drivers Study

As founder of my company, Value Growth Institute, I've noted that according to recent statistics[1], privately-held businesses or small businesses account for half the gross domestic products and employment in this country. As a result, I established the Business Value Drivers Study (BVDS) and launched an ongoing research study to help small businesses make effective decisions in creating value in their businesses for the owners and society alike.

The Business Value Drivers Study (BVDs) is the first comprehensive and situationally based investigation of tension of mission critical activities (MCAs) for business owners. The study, deployed May 2010, specifically examined each of the mission critical activities. The BVDS looks at the tension level of each mission critical activity and provides suggestions on untapped potential opportunities in any given activity among the study group.

---

[1] U.S. Small Business Administration Office of Advocacy FAQ http://web.sba.gov/faqs/faqIndexAll.cfm?areaid=24

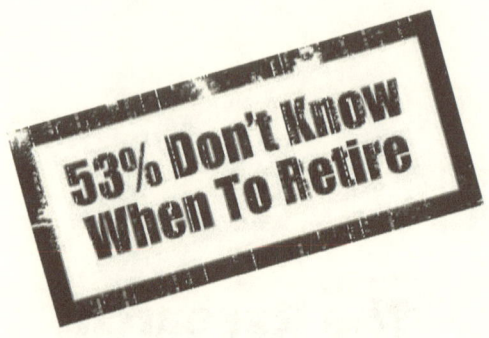

It is my desire that the interviews of this Business Value Drivers (BVD) study demonstrate how any business owner can complete Mission Critical Activities (MCAs). I hope this helps all business owners increase their ability, challenge themselves and drive themselves toward building value in their business—value that matters in their own personal life goals. With this foundation, along with proper discipline, accountability and structure, any business owner can build the value they deserve from their business and realize their dreams.

What Drives Business Value?

The majority of business owners will tell you they are in business because they want to make more money and gain financial independence. Over the years, I have seen many successful business owners create value in their businesses, and thus, for themselves, by focusing on *mission-critical* activities.

Are you creating the value in your business needed to make financial independence a reality? How can you know if what you are doing will ultimately lead to this goal? Not every business owner has the insight, knowledge or intuition to recognize what will boost the value of his or her company without training.

But is owning and operating a successful[2] business a skill that can be learned or trained? I think so, and have created this look at business success stories designed to help small businesses make effective decisions in creating value in their businesses. It is my wish that the value extends beyond business and becomes meaningful to society as well. But that is up to you.

In the BVD Study, I found that most business owners, regardless of their current success are:

- Not aware of untapped growth or value creation potential
- Settling for less-than-ideal results in the current environment
- Limiting risk-taking in their leadership role

Did you start your business with an end in mind? And the end doesn't have to mean *retirement*. The end is the vision you have for where you want your business to take you—whether that means the financial independence to start another business, participate fulltime in a community endeavor, or have the time to watch your children and grandchildren grow. That call is yours. But creating business value is the first step. It doesn't matter if you have been in business for many, many years or just getting started, start building business value now.

Based on my recent study, the majority of the BVDS participants should take the following steps to create value in their business:

- Get more training or information
- Create more challenge
- Harness more drive

---

[2] Bartiromo, Maria. 2010. The 10 laws of enduring success. Crown Business.

Chia-Li Chien

What do *you* need to do to create value in your business and change your life and the world around you as well? Read on and find out how you can start making changes toward what really matters to you.

What Makes the BVD Study Valuable to You?

As you are most likely aware, Facebook went public in May 2012. That meant Mark Zuckerberg, Founder, Chairman and CEO of Facebook had the potential to reach a personal net worth north of $14.7 billion[3]—just in time for his 28th birthday in May.

Many people have become instant millionaires or even billionaires as the result of IPOs, and Mark Zuckerberg is no exception. When talking to or interviewing entrepreneurs, I often ask, "What does your end game look like in terms of your exit strategy?" Almost 95% of them, to my surprise, will tell me, "I am not ready to retire yet." Please note, I said nothing about *retirement*.

---

[3] Mark Zuckerberg From Wikipedia, the free encyclopedia http://en.wikipedia.org/wiki/Mark_Zuckerberg

Do you think Mark Zuckerberg was planning to retire after Facebook went public? As matter of fact, Jeff Bezos, CEO of Amazon did *not* retire after his company's IPO. Neither did Tony Hsieh, CEO of Zappos after he sold Zappos to Amazon. Many privately held business owners continue to work in the same business after selling their firm, regardless to whom they sell.

Business Succession Ratio

In my experience, one-third of all privately-held businesses simply close when the business owner is ready or forced to step out. One-third transfer within to other partners, family members, or children. One-third sell to a third party[4]. **Do yourself a favor—set a goal to have the opportunity to CASH OUT. Reward yourself for your hard work!** DO NOT let yourself be a part of the one-third that walks away with nothing to show for the years they put into their business.

In general, you either transfer your business internally or externally. In some cases, businesses can be structured so that they have a combination of internal and external transfers to achieve ultimate wealth for the entrepreneurs.

How many transfer methods are available for a privately-held business?

There are twenty-seven transfer methods[5] available for a privately-held business. (Please see Appendix 6)

---

[4] Brown, John H. 2006. How to Run Your Business so You Can Leave It in Style. Business Enterprise Press. Golden, Colorado.

[5] Chien, Chia-Li. 2010..Show Me The Money: Run Your Business like a Prosperous Investor. iUniverse, Inc. New York.

Exit Triggers

In my experience most privately-held business owners think about "exit," "transfer" or "sell" from one of the following event triggers[6]:

- Health problems
- Emotional and physical fatigue and feeling of being drained from owning the business. The owner has gotten bored, lost the fire, or simply doesn't have enough fight to face another economic cycle
- Family situations, such as spousal pressure to retire, divorce, children asking for ownership or employees believing the owner is not forward thinking or progressive enough
- Capital was required to take the company to the next level, or the owner felt he or she had hit a wall
- Too much competition or company was struggling

---

[6] Brown, John H. 2006. How to Run Your Business so You Can Leave It in Style. Business Enterprise Press. Golden, Colorado.

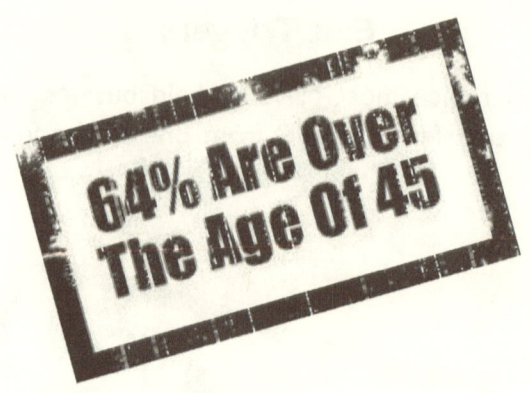

Low Priority On Exit Planning

64% of the participants in the BVD study are over the age of 45, however, 9% (of total participants) show interest in planning for the exit. This explains why the majority of owners are reactive to the word *exit*. There always seem to be an onslaught of conflicting priorities in a business, unless the business is in a very stable stage.

Most owners will not take advantage of the known methods to increase value. In the BVD study, I also found that lack of understanding of these methods contributes to a reactive exit, resulting from the triggers we just discussed, or other situations.

My findings from the BVDS indicate the majority of business owners need to learn more about each mission critical activity and effectively implement suggested changes into their business to achieve *value creation*.

These findings reveal the need for business owners to re-group, re-think and re-plan if they want to truly work toward reward. This book is to help show you how to do just that.

Chapter 1

Risk vs. Reward

I have found, without exception, that entrepreneurs are risk takers. And I suppose I'm one of them. I went on my first whitewater rafting trip in 2011. But there was a huge risk for me in making this trip.

I don't swim.

To minimize my risk, I wanted to sit closest to the guide. In addition, just to double-check my safety, I asked my daughter (you can see her in the front of the raft) to go on the trip with me. She's a Girl Scout and certified in these types of extreme outdoor sports. She was my additional safety net.

We were on Nantahala River, the coldest river in the Appalachian gorge in North Carolina. The entire run was two hours on the water, through many heart-pounding rapids, extreme moments of excitement, getting splashed and soaking wet, along with much laughter. I even sustained a hard hit from a hanging tree branch along the riverbank. Lee (our guide) tried to warn me with a "Watch out!" just two seconds before I saw it, but it was too late. Luckily I did not get knocked out of the raft.

The objective of the trip was to navigate to our destination of the 9-foot Nantahala Falls, stay in the boat and enjoy the trip.

There were many boats on the river that day, some without a Lee to guide their raft, and many of those rafts got stuck on the riverbank or hopelessly stranded on the rocks sticking out of the river. I asked Lee why these boats didn't have a rafting guide like him.

"People want to save money and go down this river on their own. Unfortunately, only the experienced guides know the river well enough to maneuver and navigate toward the finish line successfully," answered Lee.

Although a business exit can be triggered by different factors, the value varies depending on the exit methods. You must make sure all factors are working in your favor when cashing out—just like when Facebook made their IPO.

Even if you cash out due to the need for capital to expand your business you still must a have right guide. Why? Just like my whitewater rafting trip, with the right guide, I successfully reached my destination safely and claimed my reward for the day—in this case, FUN.

Yes, think of exiting your business as claiming your reward. Claim that reward and compensate yourself for the risk you took in creating and running your business. Don't wait too long or you could be faced with the triggers that might potentially decrease the value of your business.

Perhaps you don't want to or need to be a Mark Zuckerberg, CEO of Facebook. But doesn't it make sense to plan ahead for the wellbeing of your business, you and your family? Think about it—what does your end game look like in terms of an exit strategy?

In my BVD study report, there are specific value creation methods that help owners gain insights on how to avoid unfavorable exit triggers and proactively and intentionally build their business in value. Let's first look at what investors and buyers are looking for. Then, I'll illustrate how you can build your business in value to create a win-win situation for all parties.

Do yourself a favor—set a goal to be able to sell anytime! Profitably! Make it a win-win for you and your buyers/investors.

Chapter 2

What impacts business value from an investor or buyer perspective?

I'll answer that question with another question—what are the three major factors impacting real estate value, marketability and desirability[7]?

LOCATION

LOCATION

LOCATION

That's right, and I'm sure everyone has heard this before. However, let's ask ourselves now—

What are the three major factors impacting privately-held businesses?

---

[7] Slee, Robert T. 2010. Live Presentation: How to Turn Your Business Into Gold? Charlotte, NC. http://chialichien.com/cal/blog/309-how-to-turn-your-business-into-gold.html

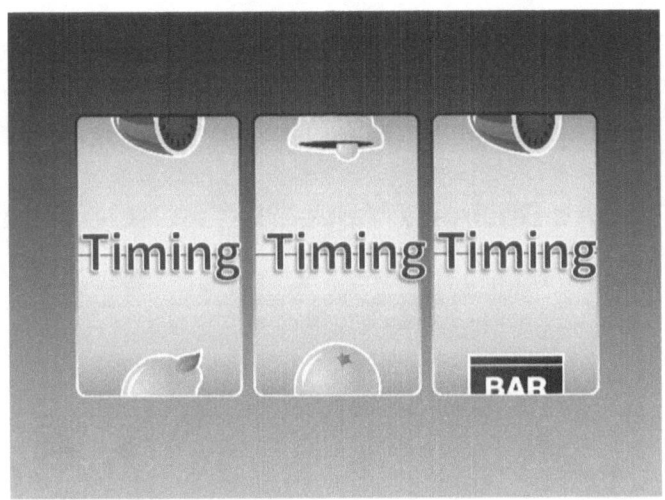

The first type of timing is Personal Timing; mostly triggered by health problems, emotional and physical fatigue and feeling of being drained from owning the business. You may be bored, have no fire in your belly or simply can't muster enough strength to face another economic cycle. A family situation, such as spousal pressure to retire, divorce, children who want to take ownership or employees who think you aren't as forward thinking, progressive, etc. as you should be can add to the pressure.

Secondly, you must consider Business Timing. Is your business mature enough to have the VALUE to create and ensure your financial independence?

Third, consider Economic Timing. What economic cycle are you currently in? In the other words—when is the right time to cash out *profitably*?

Do yourself a favor—set a goal to be able to sell anytime! Profitably! Make it a win-win for you and your buyers/investors.

For the past twenty years, investment banker Rob Slee has studied the privately-held business buy and sell cycle. He revealed the following pattern in **Midas Marketing**[8] published in 2009:

Historic Business Value 10-Yr-Cycle Chart

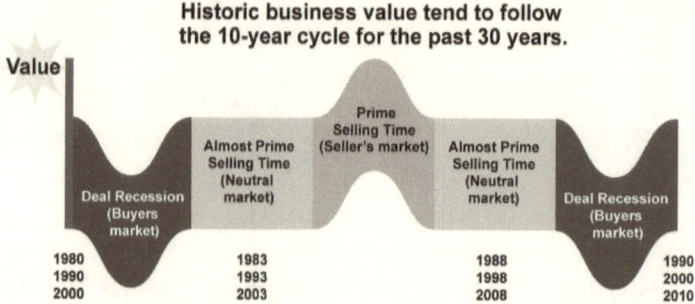

This cycle correlates with the U.S. economic cycle. According to Slee, investment bankers will typically buy companies in distress around the third or fourth years in business and sell them about the eighth year or so. Accordingly, if we as business owners can predict the prime time to cash out for maximum value, why not plan in conjunction with this cycle?

The goal is to be able to sell at any time! Profitably![9]

---

[8] Slee, Robert T. 2009. Midas Marketing, how Midas managers make markets. Charlotte, NC: Burn the Boats Press

[9] Warrillow, John. 2011. Built to Sell: Creating a Business That Can Thrive Without You. Portfolio.

This requires your business to have fundamental value for acquisition. As a value strategist, as long as my clients know their goals, I always plan "backward" for them, first uncovering what their investors or buyers will be looking for. The goal for you, the business owner, is simple—provide whatever the buyers or investors WANT! Build your business toward what they are seeking! Then it becomes a win-win for both parties.

Then what impacts business value? What impacts how you will make more money as a business owner than you would have otherwise? From an investor and buyer perspective, it's not only about, say, your technology or market position.

It's about ROI! Plain and simple!

Here's the question again. What makes a business valuable from investors' or buyers' perspectives? There are three major categories that impact business value[10]:

1. Increase recast EBITDA[11]
2. Reduce risk
3. Employ high-yield capital

I call the above actions *Business Financial Behaviors*. These three major categories of business financial behaviors are matched with the BVD study Mission Critical Activities as follows:

---

[10] Kenneth H. Marks, Robert T. Slee, Christian W. Blees, Michael R. Nall. 2012. Middle Market M & A: Handbook for Investment Banking and Business Consulting. Wiley Finance. New Jersey.

[11] Lober, Rosalie. 2009. Run Your Business Like a Fortune 100: 7 Principles for Boosting PROFITS. Wiley.

Chapter 3

BVD study Mission Critical Activities

Business Financial Behaviors Goals To Increase Business Value	BVD study Mission Critical Activities
Increase recast EBITDA	BVD_01:Earning profit on every client
	BVD_02:Earning profit on every product or service
	BVD_05:Sustaining predictable revenue source
	BVD_06:Sustaining Pull marketing (Doors swings in your way)
	BVD_07:Leveraging marketing space for maximum sales
	BVD_08:Determining the return on investment (ROI) of every productive employee

	BVD_09: Evaluating ROI with each employee and team
	BVD_11: Streamlining processes with maximum efficiency
	BVD_12: Leveraging technologies to systematize processes
	BVD_13: Positioning processes to generate profit
	BVD_14: Implementing a set of Key Performance indicators (KPI)
	BVD_15: Maintaining healthy profit margin
	NJ_08: Deploy measurable process to monitor business strategy
Reduce Risk	BVD_03: Diversifying revenue from products or services mix
	BVD_10: Developing synergy among key management team
	NJ_01: Determine the right market value of your business
	NJ_02: Determine when to exit your business
	NJ_03: Replicate your current income for the next 20 to 30 years
	NJ_04: Convert the value of your business into cash

	NJ_05: Identify key value drivers for your business
	NJ_06: Transfer your business in the most tax efficient way
	NJ_07: Maintaining healthy profit margin even if something were to happen to you or your business
Employ additional high yielding capital	BVD_04: Diversifying client base

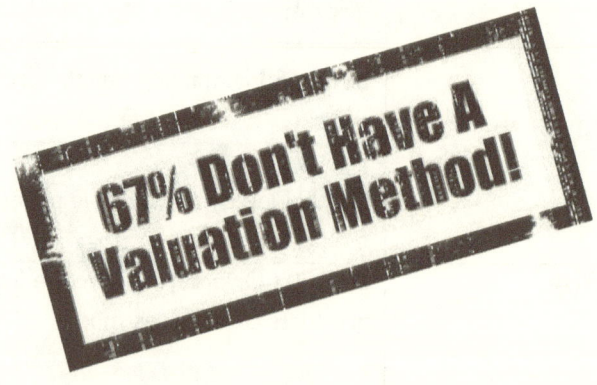

A Closer Look at What Impacts Business Value

Remember, there are three major categories that impact business value:

1. Increase recast EBITDA
2. Reduce risk
3. Employ high-yield capital.

EBITDA stands for Earnings Before Interest, Taxes, Depreciation and Amortization. It's an accounting term and used commonly in business transactions. If your annual business revenue is more than

$5MM, then EBITDA times multiples are commonly used. In anything less than $5MM[12], cash flow is often considered instead of EBITDA.

Multiples are determined by the current market condition. The multiples reflect U.S. economic conditions as well as the volume of transactions in privately-held businesses buy/sell activities.

Increase Recast EBITDA

The Value Drivers to increase recast EBITDA include:

1. Increase sales
2. Lower cost of goods sold
3. Control operating expenses

The BVD Study reveals the top three mission critical activities of each business in the value goals category worth a closer look from all business owners.

	Increase recast EBITDA		Reduce Risk
1	BVD_08: Determining the return on investment (ROI) of every productive employee (71%)	1	NJ_06: Transfer your business in the most tax efficient way (81%)
2	BVD_13: Positioning processes to generate profit (70%)	2	NJ_04: Convert the value of your business into cash (80%)

---

[12] Chien, Chia-Li. 2010. What's Your $1 Million Business Worth? http://chialichien.com/cal/resources/published-articles/125-whats-your-1-million-business-worth.html

| 3 | BVD_09: Evaluating ROI with each employee and team (67%) | 3 | NJ_07: Maintaining healthy profit margin even if something were to happen to you or your business (75%) |

What are ways you can increase sales, ultimately increasing business value and the chance to cash out with financial independence? One of the most practical strategies to increase sales is to enter a niche market.

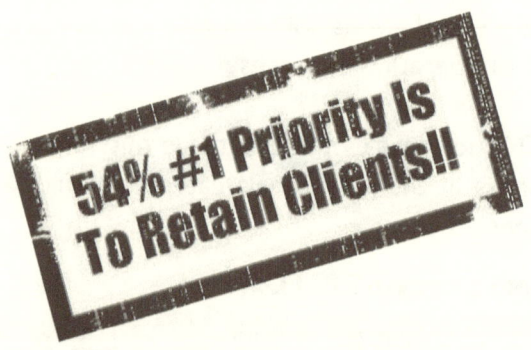

Karen's real estate company is a New York-based office rental agency. They opened in 2007, right before the real estate crisis began in 2008. They decided to locate in a co-working space, which had been established for many years, dominated by big real estate companies such as Regis and franchised companies like OfficeSuite[13]. To compete and increase their sales, Karen entered a niche in which her office space could function as both a community for women business owners ripe with learning opportunities and a physical co-working space where women could come to work meet and learn. By 2010, they expanded to an additional floor to accommodate increasing demand.

---

[13] Gansky, Lisa. 2010. The Mesh: Why the Future of Business is Sharing by Lisa Gansky. Portfolio.

Have you ever heard the saying, "**Niche is rich?**[14]" As you reevaluate your business and its value, check out your competitors and see if you are niched well enough to continue to increase sales regardless of economic conditions.

But let's get to the question that is really bothering you—"What are the *risks* in working toward increasing my business value?"

Reduce Risk

The BVD Study indicated three top mission critical activities in each business value goals category that make it worth changing tasks or that can simply raising the bar.

	Increase recast EBITDA		**Reduce Risk**
1	BVD_09:Evaluating ROI with each employee and team (67%)	1	NJ_05:Identify key value drivers for your business (62%)
2	BVD_06:Sustaining Pull marketing (doors swings in your way) (67%)	2	NJ_06:Transfer your business in the most tax efficient way (59%)
3	BVD_11:Streamlining processes with maximum efficiency (67%)	3	NJ_02:Determine when to exit your business (59%)

Value Drivers to **reduce risk** include:

---

[14] Kennedy, Dan S.; Jason Marrs (2011). No B.S. Price Strategy: The Ultimate No Holds Barred Kick Butt Take No Prisoner Guide to Profits, Power, and Prosperity . Entrepreneur Press.

1. Reduce business risk
2. Reduce cost of capital
3. Reduce customer concentration
4. Have a key management team

What are ways to reduce business risk? One practical strategy to reduce business risk is to **benchmark higher than your competitors**.

Mary's company had been in the Top 50 Fastest Growing Companies in the U.S. for two years in a row. In late 2008, when so many commercial banks were calling in their lines of credit business (since the banks too wanted to reduce their risk), Mary was one of many small businesses that lost that type of financial lifeline. She was in a panic and anxious to find anyone who could provide her a line of credit. She went to several commercial banks, but no one was even willing to take her application, except for one local community bank. Let's name this community bank ABC.

Mary needed to maintain her $1MM line of credit in order to continue to fill her orders. Bank ABC required Mary to deposit $2MM cash as collateral before she could obtain the line of credit. (We're all scratching our heads at this point, because WE understand that if Mary had $2MM cash, she wouldn't need the $1MM line of credit.) She ended up with a type of alternative financing from a non-bank financial institution. After several months and heavy fees from this non-bank (let's name them XYZ), XYZ told Mary that due to her high customer concentration that exceeded the industry benchmark by 50%, they could only provide $500K line of credit instead of $1MM.

In the end, Mary finally re-established her line of credit and continued to fill orders and grow her business. Sadly, she continues to be below the industry benchmark when it comes to the most critical financial ratio that every financial institution, investor or buyer is looking for. Despite continued success in revenue growth, unless she works on what's important in her company, she just won't have the value investors or buyers are looking for when she is ready to exit and cash out.

Employ High-Yield Capital

Value Drivers to *employ additional high-yield capital* include:

1. Improve investment decisions
2. Decrease capital base

What are ways to decrease capital base? One of the practical strategies to decrease capital base is to disengage under-performing business, product lines or customers.

Cindy has a company that primarily provides commercial renovation services. Over the years, she saw opportunities decline, and prior to the 2008 financial crisis, she decided to shed declining and underperforming sales and product lines.

Then, she decided to enter LEED Projects[15] and LEED Waste Management as a provider. As most commercial real estate business came to a halt nationwide, the impact on her company was no different than that of other companies. No different except for the fact that all her competitors went out of business, and she continued to slowly absorb the market share as one of the few LEED companies certified to do the type of work her company does. To my knowledge, she is one of the very few highly specialized (niched) firms in her state and continues to have secure footing in her market place.

---

[15] Pensak, David. 2008. Innovation for underdogs : how to make the leap from what if to now what. Career Press.

Chapter 4

Selected Interviews from the BVD Study

I've selected seven worthwhile businesses that I believe all business owners can learn from. These businesses are not only in the top 3% of all small businesses, but also worthy of duplication if you're in the same industries.

I CAN DO BETTER!

Building Emotional Capital in Your Business

Why you should and how it can lead to business success.

"I can do better!" thought Victor Zhang, while an engineer at FoxConn (global computer, communication and consumer-electronics leaders) at age 24. He saw the massive market opportunities in electronic connectors, especially in the molding business, and launched his business TSP Industrial Co., Ltd. (aka TSP) in 1999. Today, Mr. Zhang employs well over 600 employees globally and has three manufacturing plants in China.

Their products sustain the precision to tolerance of 0.001mm and very likely no end-users such as you or I will ever see them. Yet what they build plays a crucial part in the success of final products in consumer electronics, automobile electronics, aerospace, computer manufacturing, medical electronics and even home appliances.

"We are in the people business," says Mr. Zhang. "Building and maintaining a TRUST relationship is in everything we do. My employees are my family," he emphasizes, passionate about motivating his team to self-actualization or to realizing their full potential. "Work or business is just a platform that allows my family/team to reach their full potential in life," Mr. Zhang says enthusiastically. Although he initially started his company to gain financial freedom, over time his vision and passion acted as a solid guide toward becoming the successful business it is today.

Such a successful business in the vibrant Chinese market also comes with challenges. Mr. Zhang and his team proactively provide solutions to their market and industry. But there are three particular challenges Mr. Zhang faces today:

1. Talent Shortages

I naively always want to think China has abundant resources—especially people! It's interesting to hear Mr. Zhang contradict this belief. The U.S. faces the same talent shortages in technology areas. Skilled talent is hard to come by wherever you are, and these employees make up 60% of Mr. Zhang's workforce. Although there is no shortcut in addressing the need for talent as a resource, Mr. Zhang deploys intensive internal training as well as external talent scouting such as *name your class*.

Mr. Zhang strategically partnered with two local community colleges in 2011, each with an average of 45 students majoring in mechanical or molding engineering. It's not just an internship; these groups of students get to go through his company's culture training too.

These students, who are also potential employees, receive first-hand knowledge and how to apply it in the company's culture as part of their internship experience. When they receive their degree, they are ready to enter the TSP workforce with raw learned technical skills as well as carefully designed soft skills from TSP. What a brilliant program Mr. Zhang has implemented! (We all understand that soft skills are not something you can go to school for. Real life environments—especially at a younger age that give you a head start—make a whole world of difference.) This future talent base can leverage Mr. Zhang's platform and as a result find better career choices and lifestyles.

2. Global Expansion

Through carefully planned global expansion, today Mr. Zhang has sales offices in Japan, the USA and Europe. Global opportunities sometime mean gaps in the way his team can communicate with prospects or new customers. Communication gaps include language, culture (Western vs. Chinese) and interpersonal interactions. The localization of their sales force in Japan, the USA and Europe paves the way for Mr. Zhang's team to greatly reduce these gaps over time.

3. Timeless Sustainability Legacy

Through a self-discovery process, Mr. Zhang converted to Buddhism in 2004. Buddhism in China and the rest of Asia essentially encompasses religion, Tao philosophy, Chinese traditions, beliefs, and practices. In the practice of *Zen*, Mr. Zhang systematically duplicates himself in his management teams and sees himself as a business architect in order to create his business platform. A platform enables his workforce to realize their potential in life and subsequently create a better community.

Numbers don't drive business performance alone—it's the people! People are the emotional capital that you should aim to invest in. Your team ultimately will take your business to your vision. Your investment in your team starts with you the owner. As I've interviewed many successful business owners around the world, I find that many are much like Mr. Zhang. Their motive is no longer to achieve financial freedom for themselves. Their motive is achieving maximum positive impact in the communities in which the business operates.

Whether you're Protestant Christian, Catholic, Muslim, Buddhist—whatever your religious beliefs—as a business owner, you are not just a business leader but also a spiritual guide. How you motivate your people beyond projects, money and incentives will be evident in your emotional capital performance. And only your workforce can measure that performance—not you. That performance yields how successfully your business will continue on the path of your desired vision.

"DO YOU HAVE SCALABLE BUSINESS MODEL!"

How Will You Scale Your Business And Build Value?

Identify resources that will yield substantial value creation.

We're in the Aggregation Age! The Aggregation Age marks the ability of a business to leverage intellectual property on a scalable platform. The business owns minimum resources with tightly controlled processes over profits, human capital and integrated supply chain, yielding substantial value creation for the owners.

Mr. Gregory J. Tigani, President of Northwest Companies, has deployed a plug-and-play business model since 2008. The Northwest Companies have grown organically an average of 25% annually for the past three years, while most businesses have struggled to survive in tough economic conditions.

The Northwest Companies essentially have been in business since 1984. In 2008, it acquired Northwest Landscape Management Inc. and Northwest Snow Management Inc., then merged the two companies and implemented strategies to scale the business and broaden the market and verticals to the place things are today. In the first full year of operations, the company more than tripled the top line revenue from operations and had expanded its service footprint from a 9-state region to over 40 states with operations. Today it operates in 48 states and continues to expand its client base nationally.

Northwest Companies services corporations with multiple locations, such as restaurant chains, banks, regional daycare centers, hospitals and utility companies. Most of their customers are Fortune 500 firms. They handle exterior facilities management as well as exterior facilities development and snow management.

Mr. Tigani leverages one of their intellectual properties, a Service Reporting System (SRS), which provides real-time status and reporting to his customers, as well as manages subcontractors in job delivery. At the time of this writing, the Northwest Companies had 32 employees and 1,200 sub-contractors (per 1099 info). Mr. Tigani is projecting to more than double his business by 2015. That means double the number of employees and triple the number of sub-contractors.

A tight control on niche, relationships, cost, risk and processes on a scalable platform allows Mr. Tigani to grow in substantial value without diminishing the capital base. Within a system that scales this well, he is able to maintain or even increase the level of performance or efficiency when tested by larger operational demands. (In a corporate sense, a scalable company can maintain or improve profit margins while sales volume increases.)

With a one-year long sales cycle, Mr. Tigani's sales team has a full pipeline to bring in works beyond their current capacity. Their supply chain is equipped with a streamlined subcontractors vetting process. It allows them to build up top quality inventory to fulfill customer contracts. With a three-tier structure for service providers or subcontractors, the better subcontractors perform the more protected stream of income for these small businesses. Each of these small businesses or subcontractors has a minimum of 12 people on their team.

Essentially, Northwest Companies takes care of all sales and marketing for these subcontractors. This powerful platform not only creates jobs throughout the U.S. but also provides attractive buying power for any of their supplies, such as premium Anti/De-icing Clean Tech products. Not to my surprise, another global player in the industry is currently using the SRS. Absolutely brilliant!!

Mr. Tigani has five children, is a cancer survivor and an ex-executive of Jefferies & Company. He relies on his deep roots of M&A leadership experience to successfully scale his business. His wealth of knowledge and experience in measuring business success, its structure and team, has allowed him to create this successful venture in a very short time. As a business architect, Mr. Tigani humbly credits his success through active learning in leadership, operations and strategy.

"My goal as the visionary and CEO of the company is to provide sustainability of the organization through the leveraging of systems, technology and skilled management," says Mr. Tigani. His focus in human capital development creates a solid foundation of management infrastructure, which allows him to scale rapidly.

Leveraging Mr. Tigani's core competencies, including a good judge of character[16], trusting his instinct in management, knowing daily cash reserve position and being proactive in actions from Key Performance Indicators truly make him the ultimate solutions guy. He has become an expert in the business of substantial VALUE creation (by my estimation of more than 5X of current value).

Mr. Tigani recommends three critical success factors for all entrepreneurs:

- Build great customer relationships beyond the current network and consciously diversify your customer base
- Leverage competencies and dedicated talents or human capital, including employees and subcontractors
- Control value growth without diminishing capital base

Just like any other great investor, Mr. Tigani is already planning beyond 2015. His vision is to put more companies like Northwest Companies in his future venture portfolio. With solid customer relations, substantial financial value (from the investors' point of view) and management infrastructure (from employees/contractors' perspective), this secret and powerful Triple Bottom Line formula solidly exists on the scalable platform Mr. Tigani has created.

It is not IF— it is WHEN—can a business owner exit profitably on his or her own terms? I want to remind all privately-held owners out there to take a closer look at your own business(es). Regardless of the performance of your Triple Bottom Line formula, you must you look beyond three years into the future.

---

[16] Huntsman, Jon M. 2008. Winners Never Cheat: : Even in Difficult Times. Pearson Prentice Hall.

Have you done that yet? If yes, what is your definition of substantial VALUE creation from your business? And can it actually meet or exceed your financial independence expectations? If your business is not built on a scalable platform, then how will you build it in value in order to embark on your NEXT JOURNEY®?

STRIVING FOR EXCELLENCE

Striving For Excellence In Every Aspect Of Life And Business

The Benham brothers set an example for every business owner.

What does a typical famous sports figure usually do after retirement from sports[17]? Well, David and Jason Benham, the famous identical twin brothers who retired from the St. Louis Cardinals, know their path with more clarity than anyone else.

---

[17] Lewis, Michael. 2003. Moneyball: The Art of Winning an Unfair Game. W. W. Norton & Company.

"God favors and opens the doors, but business excellence keeps you there!" said Jason Benham. Both brothers strive for excellence in every aspect in life including business, family, community and spirituality. See below for a timeline of accomplishments from the team best known as the Benham Brothers of the BENHAM Companies.

- 2001: Retired from St. Louis Cardinals
- 2002 to 2003: Market research in real estate business
- 2004: Formed BENHAM Real Estate Group; A Real Estate Broker niche in foreclosure
- 2005: Formed an Entity 2 in Property Management Firm
- 2007: Franchised BENHAM REO Group; Sold Entity 2 with profit **[Exit 1] [Exit 2]**
- 2009: Formed Entity 3 "shared service" outsourcing; BENHAM Foundation **[Exit 3]**
- 2010: BENHAM REO Group reached 100 offices; Merged with Flatworld Solutions **[Exit 4]**
- 2012: ThereIsMore.com TRUE wealth Movement

<u>Spotting a need and meeting a need.</u> The Benhams began to notice billboards with messages such as, "Bankrupt OK," or "Zero money down to move you into your dream home." Even while already involved in conducting typical real estate transactions, the Benham brothers had spotted a need in the marketplace in 2003. They knew the type of billboard messaging they were seeing targeted renters and putting those renters into homeownership despite a probable lack of understanding of the then-popular adjustable rate mortgages.

The brother team wondered what banks would do if they had an influx of inventories they needed to liquidate. At the time, the answer from the banks was, "That'll never happened, and even if it did, we'll have real estate brokers sell it for us." Once the brothers had identified the potential, they specialized their business in liquidation and foreclosure properties for banks.

Leveraging Market Makers[18]. In addition to the niche market the Benham brothers entered in the real estate industry, they leveraged and built solid relationships with their market makers. *Market makers are entities that have exactly your ideal target customers* (in their case, domestic banks). The Benham brothers became a key relationship management tool for the market makers in their business.

Capitalizing on their know how – The now formidable real estate team began to automate liquidation and foreclosure management and tracking processes. "**Process before profits**," vowed David Benham, when they knew they had to have the ability to process 40 foreclosure properties as fast as 400. They intuitively knew to put a system in place that could manage all details of foreclosure properties with tracking. Why? Their brand promise was to handle liquidation for banks in a quarter of the time of any other brokers in town. Having a solid system as a foundation allows them to **speed to response** with every bank they work with, regardless of the profitability of the properties.

"*I never thought about exit strategy before*," David Benham told me during my third annual BVD study/interview with them. (They learned that term while filling out the on-line BVD assessment.) If you take a close look at the timeline above, you will notice the Benham brothers had already at this point used four different exit/transfer methods without realizing it.

Scale the business model with a solid foundation to handle volume. The Benham brothers have leveraged their solid proprietary online business management system, which they can scale easily. They

---

[18] Maney, Kevin. 2010. Trade-off : why some things catch on, and others don't. Crown Business.

franchised their business model in 2007, using one of twenty-even exit strategy methods mentioned earlier in this book. (You can see all twenty-seven exit/transfer methods in Appendix 6):

Transfer Channels	Internal Transfer				External Transfer		
	Employees	Charitable Trusts	Family	Co-Owners	Outside (Retire)	Outside (Continue)	Public
Transfer Methods	ESOPs	Charitable Remainder Trusts	Outright Gifts	Buy/Sell	Negotiated	Consolidate	Initial Public Offerings
	Management Buyouts/Ins	Charitable Lead Trusts	SCINs	Russian Roulette	One-Step Private Auctions	Roll-ups	Direct Public Offerings
	Phantom Stock		Annuities	Dutch Auction	Two-Step Private Auctions	Buy and Build	Reverse Mergers
	Stock appreciation Rights		GRATs	Right of First Refusal		ReCap	Going Private
			FLPs				
			IDGTs				

1) *External Transfer—Outside (Continued)*. Credit their solid foundation of a system or their *know how*, but within two and a half years, the brothers had reached the mark of 100 offices nationwide. (See **Exit 1** in above)

Meanwhile, the Benham brothers knew to stay *focused on only investing in their core competency.* They used another of the twenty-seven exit strategy methods: 2) *External Transfer—Outside (Retire)*. They profitably sold an entity that was not their core competency. (See **Exit 2** in above)

In 2009, the Benhams used another one of the twenty-seven exit strategy methods: 3) *Internal Transfer—Charitable Trusts* to create the BENHAM Foundation that allows them to continue on their *Reverse Missioneering* quest to spread their spirituality message around the globe. (See **Exit 3 in** above) They *re-circulate* portions of their profit back into the *local community* where their facility is located. They currently have one model company fully functioning with seventy-five employees in Davao City, Philippines. They will soon to break ground on a Ghana location.

In 2010, they used another of the twenty-seven exit strategy methods: 4) ***External Transfer—Outside (Continued),*** by merging their *shared service outsourcing* entity with Flatworld Solutions. (See **Exit 4** in the above)

If you are like me, you are by now wondering how the Benham brothers always knew what to do and how to be continuously successful in all aspects of life. They humbly credit their success to their father, Flip Benham, who leads the Kerygma Church in Concord, NC.

"My father taught me everything in life; not to be just a business man, but to be a biblical thinker," Jason Benham says. Because of their devotion to their purpose and passion in life to *make an impact*, they created and still follow the three core values of Benham Companies:

- Produce value
- Be faithful in the little things
- Breathe life

These three core values are the calipers used to measure the BENHAM Company's success. David Benham is a father of five and married to Lori. Jason Benham is a father of four and married to Tori. They have already started passing on their beliefs to their children by not only getting them involved in their philanthropy efforts but also these core values. The couples strive to position the next generation for continuous success in life as well as for making an impact in the world.

The Benham brothers drive their business value upward by consistently re-aligning the three business value factors, which include 1) personal timing 2) business timing and 3) economic timing. They stay true to their three core values and use them as the *rules* for their journey.

Along the way, they are leveraging as many exit/transfer strategy methods as possible to properly claim their reward by compensating themselves for the risk they took in creating and running their businesses. Meanwhile, they continue to *re-circulate* portions of the profit back into the local community where their businesses operate.

"Exit" is neither a bad word nor about losing your social status or damaging the ego. It's merely a means to re-position yourself for your NEXT JOURNEY®! With several business entities, the Benham brothers had already used four different exit/transfer methods without realizing it. Think about it—how many exit/transfer methods can you use in your business(es) so that you too can properly claim your reward in compensation for the risk you took in creating and running your business(es)? Perhaps, like the Benham brothers, you too can be a part of or create a movement to better our community at the same time.

YOUR SUCCESS DEPENDS ON YOUR VISION!

Creating A Mission Statement That Drives Your Success

How one business owner turned his passion and purpose into a successful business.

Do you have a mission statement? Are you thinking in terms of your *business* mission statement? Or do you have two statements—one personal and another for business—or only one tightly aligned mission statement?

> *To help people become leaders and achieve the success they desire.*

Early in his career, at age 24 to be exact, Tim developed the above aligned personal and business mission statement. Today, Tim Flanagan's company, H.F. Financial, ranks in the top three largest area financial planning firms of 2011 in Charlotte. Tim is the 4th CEO in this 3rd generation family business, which has been in operation since 1935. Tim's passion for helping people and seeing people succeed is his internal driver for continuous success in a complex, highly regulated financial industry.

Tim's father has been his greatest influence. He put Tim on the path of personal development early. Tim went through the **7 Habits of Highly Effective People**[19] and became leadership-centric from the very start of his business. Tim's father let him chart his own course and come to the realization on his own that the business acts as the vehicle that allows him to grow in his personal/business mission statement. Tim is allowing his own son, a college business major, to do the same.

The common problem of conducting business in this ever-changing landscape of complex financial regulations is how to create and stick to a business model. In a franchised business model such as Tim's, there are ninety-one affiliated financial advisors acting as independent contractors working with the company. Many financial advisors (independent contractors) in the industry don't operate as if they are a business.

But like any entrepreneurial endeavor, it takes more than just a business card to sustain a healthy profit margin. The compressed margin from commissions and fees of financial products and services allow Tim to provide valued services to his financial advisors

---

[19] Covey, Stephen R. 2004. The 7 Habits of Highly Effective People. Revised edition . Free Press.

(independent contractors). These services are relevant in support of their clients.

Tim pointed out three common issues financial advisors (as entrepreneurs) face:

1. They suffer from an insufficient number of people to prospect in their own network
2. They are not given enough time to build the business and knowledge it takes to sustain the business
3. They do not have a serious commitment, perseverance and self-belief in a better future via the business vehicle

(I would say that in my experience, no matter what type of business an entrepreneur creates, these three issues are a common thread.)

To address these continuous challenges in the business model, today Tim has three solutions to organically grow his business at 10% to 12% annually:

1. Be more rigorous and selective in whom they bring in as an independent financial advisor (aka entrepreneur)
2. Test the commitment of vision of the entrepreneur's future. Continuously remind him or her of that vision with on-going guidance, encouragement and support
3. Be truthful regarding the ability to consistently bring in revenue

With 22 years in this ever-changing, regulated landscape, Tim and his team of financial planners can spot a qualified candidate at first glance. The right candidate will typically possess leadership qualities such as:

- Professional experience instead of a series of jobs

- A mission in life
- A destination goal compatible to where the business can take them
- Energized to use this business vehicle
- An engaged human being

In addition to these tactics, Tim constantly reflects on what's going on in the world and is very much focused on servicing the local vibrant affinity or ethnic communities such as Asian-Americans, African-Americans and Latino-Americans, etc. As an early adopter of this diversity trend in financial planning, Tim is building brand recognition and paying attention to each unique need in the local communities. It fast becomes evident how Tim grows his business organically.

Here are three valuable pieces of advice Tim offers every entrepreneur:

1. Invest in the right path and stay on that path
2. Expect and live in six core values: Integrity, Conviction, Accountability, Service to Others, Professionalism and Growth
3. Focus on only what's important in values, goals and aspirations

Keep your eye on the prize!

So, what's your mission statement? How aligned is your mission statement to your personal life *and* business? The passion, or your internal drive, will become obvious in any successful business. Yet it might take years to see that. No matter what business you're in, take a moment to reflect on your mission statement. Is it still driving you toward your goals? Stay focused on the path to your prize/passion/purpose and arrive at your destination in your desired timeframe.

"DISCIPLINE IS THE BRIDGE BETWEEN GOALS AND ACCOMPLISHMENTS."

How To Convert Prospects Into Customers

Leverage technology for consistent sales and follow-up.

In my first business, I was a federal minority subcontractor providing software development servicing to the energy industry. Even with only one client and one type of revenue source, I still didn't put forth any sales and marketing efforts.

So when I started my management consulting business in 2004, I had to learn how to market my business to small and mid-sized companies.

Today, as I try to grow my business, my needs for marketing and sales have evolved again. I need more sophisticated processes. So I hired an event specialist to follow-up with networking and special promotion e-mail campaigns after my speaking engagements. In so doing, I discovered that my company has multiple prospect lists: There's one in my e-mail marketing online system, one in my e-mail systems, one in my centralized online systems (mostly spreadsheets) and one in my accounting system. I must consolidate these valuable lists so I can do more business. In other words, I have to conquer the chaos.

For advice on how to do that, I turned to Clate Mask[20], also an interviewee in the Business Value Drivers (BVD) study. Co-founder and CEO of Infusionsoft, Mask is a small-business growth expert who has worked with thousands of entrepreneurs and co-authored The New York Times bestseller, Conquer the Chaos: How to Grow a Successful Small Business Without Going Crazy.

"'I wish I could clone myself' is probably the phrase most often uttered by overworked, overstressed and underpaid small-business owners," Mask says. Mask discussed some mistakes he says that prevent small businesses from growing.

1. *Lack of consistent new leads follow-up.* "Studies show that 80% of people buy between sales contact # 5 and # 12. Yet most people stop following up after attempt # 3," Mask says. Can you imagine how much it may cost your company if you do not continue following up after only three attempts?

---

[20] Mask, Clate. 2010. Conquer the Chaos: How to Grow a Successful Small Business Without Going Crazy. Wiley.

2. ***Limited post-sales follow-up***. "How many times have you purchased something, never to hear from the company again?" Mask asks. Entrepreneurs don't pay attention to repeat customers, yet it is less expensive to retain repeat customers than acquire new customers. Have you sold everything you can possibly sell to your customers?

3. ***No time for nurturing relationships***. "We all know that people buy when the time is right for them, not when you're anxious to sell," Mask says. Take time to close deals. People buy from those whom they know; use your time effectively to build that relationship.

4. ***Not getting paid on a timely basis***. I always tell clients not to finance their clients' purchases. Yet many businesses let their accounts receivable sit there until there is a cash-flow problem. Automatic billing is a great way to keep track. Then get on the phone if a client or customer hasn't paid. Don't be their bank.

5. ***Inconsistent marketing and sales process***. The worst thing that could happen in your company is to have each sales and marketing employee say different or conflicting things when working with clients or prospects. You don't have to use a script, but consistency will help your team close more deals.

To grow your business, here are three things Mask recommends you consider implementing:

1. ***Consistently spend the right amount of money and time in marketing***. Many entrepreneurs have an on-off relationship with marketing; you must have a consistent method for generating leads. Dedicate a set amount of time to marketing and market consistently.

2. **Stop trying to do everything yourself.** Entrepreneurs are proud control freaks. Most don't trust other people to do things the right way. Build an organization or surround yourself with people who can do what you're not good at doing or don't want to do. Hold them accountable to drive results. Your way may not always be the best way.

3. **Have a systematic follow-up process on a weekly basis.** Acquisition of new clients is expensive. It's more expensive if you don't follow up with your leads. Consistently reaching out to new and existing clients is crucial. Communicate effectively and stay in front of clients and prospect with value-added messages. This also shows your work ethic and business integrity.

Although I have paper processes in my company, I'm guilty (as are many businesses out there) of not having a central location for sales and marketing processes. I am now in the process of consolidating my five lists into Infusionsoft. It does take time to consolidate lists and the marketing and sales processes along with accounting systems integration. The hard work will pay off soon, though. I'm already seeing a steady sales increase, all because I have an improved system.

KNOW THE VALUE OF A CUSTOMER!

Happiness Is Not All About The Money

A Burmese immigrant builds a successful company by focusing on quality, customer service and satisfied employees.

What does a typical 8-year-old child do after school? Well, when Philip Maung was 8-years-old, he worked at his parents' fried pork belly business in Burma (the largest country by geographical area in mainland Southeast Asia) as a street vendor. He watched his parents struggle to make ends meets and to support their seven children. He saw firsthand the need to improve the lifestyle of the poor—a perspective that helped shape the man Maung is today.

Maung is CEO of Hissho Sushi—which won a ranking in the Top 100 Food & Beverage in the 2010 Inc. 5000. Based in North Carolina, Hissho Sushi is a food-service and distribution company managing and operating more than 400 sushi bars across the United States. The company's partners include Dean & DeLuca, Carolinas Medical Center and Charlotte/Douglas International Airport. Maung and his wife, Kristina, started Hissho Sushi from their dining room in 1998.

Maung's passion is to inspire people to improve their lifestyle, and his mission is to make his company a fun place to work for more than 150 employees. Many of the employees and outside contractors are refugees from Burma. As an immigrant himself, he never forgets where he came from and makes it a point to help fellow immigrants. When you walk into Hissho Sushi's 46,000-square-foot headquarters, you can see an international work force all striving to provide the best customer service in the food industry. "Happiness is not all about the money," Maung says.

Through years of working with business owners, I've come to the conclusion there are three categories of entrepreneurs: **Technician, Manager and Business Architect**:

Technician—Your business provides you a salary of less than $100,000 a year. (Please make a note here; I said "salary" not "revenue.")

Manager—Typically, you've managed to create a lifestyle in which the business provides you a salary of around $250,000 a year.

You should strive, beginning now, to become a **Business Architect**. Other than the fact that the business provides an annual salary of greater than $250,000 for the owner/architect, there is usually also a minimum of three to five times of business value back to the owner when you become the **Architect** of your business.

So how do Business Architects make it happen? Well, they most likely have deployed a *platform* with a selling relationship of many to many (M:M), as opposed to one to one (1:1). The selling relationship of M:M allows the Business Architect to focus on other important factors of the business. These factors could include maximizing value for employees, customers, investors or the innovation of processes to create or improve products (including services).

There are three basic types of selling relationships:

- **One to one (1:1)**—You sell one product/ contract/project to one customer at a time. When there is no customer, there is no income. For example, the contractor who builds a deck for a customer one at a time.
- **One to Many (1:M)**—You sell one product to many customers at a time. Or you have other sales teams selling the one product to many customers at a time. For example, a coach provides a group coaching session with many customers at the same time.
- **Many to many (M:M)**—You have many sales teams out there selling multiple products to many customers at one time on a *platform*. For example, a CRM software company deploys affiliate programs to allow many affiliates to virtually sell multiple levels of software to many customers at one time, using a pre-defined platform.

Do you remember what Amazon.com used to sell on their website in 1994? Books right? Then they effectively created a platform to allow a M:M selling relationship. Today, anyone can list their products with Amazon.com—as matter of fact—Amazon.com sells pretty much everything today.

So does that mean in order to have a M:M or platform selling business sales model you must be on-line? Not really. Take a look at fast-food franchises such as McDonald's, Burger King®, etc. A franchise is also a platform. Although Maung's business, Hissho Sushi, is not a franchise, just like many mid-sized businesses, they were already using this as a platform before they even considered franchising or licensing.

Here are some practical strategies to help move your business from a 1:1 selling relationship to M:M.

1. **Carefully define the market makers**—Base your definition on your products (including services) and market space. Each product line should naturally fit into a specific market space, therefore ensuring there is always a market maker to help you move from 1:1 to 1:M to M:M selling relationships. A Market Maker is an entity that has your exact target customers. In other words, they're well established in your market space. Market makers can include strategic alliances, specific interest trade groups, or even just another complimentary business. They are all around you.

2. **Develop a consistent marketing system**—No matter what type of marketing you currently deploy, whether on or off line, you must have a consistent marketing system in place. A system is a series of processes that allow you to consistently fill your prospect pipeline. This allows you time to continue to do what you do best. The key word here is consistent; most entrepreneurs engage in marketing strategies and tactics when they have finished up their last 1:1 job. A consistent system will allow your market makers to successfully market or sell on your behalf.

3. **Develop a Platform**—Take a look at your existing products, customers and suppliers. Could you leverage what you currently have and duplicate that process to become a platform? A platform allows others to market/sell for you. Fundamentally, this is a strategic

move to allow your business not only to create tremendous value, but also to grow revenue in a non-incremental way.

Despite the economic downturn, Hissho Sushi continues to grow. What can we learn from this Business Architect and fast-growing company?

* **Align with the right market makers.** As you recall, a market maker is an entity or person that has your exact target customers or clients. Maung is focused on high-quality products, so he only aligns with market makers who share that focus. Dean & DeLuca is just one of his market makers.

* **Be a partner, not a vendor.** Maung's goal is to create a win-win situation for any relationship. He positions his company as a partner, not just another supplier or vendor. His partnerships with many market makers have blossomed because he proactively addresses his business partners' needs.

* **Focus on what the industry is lacking—customer service**[21]. Hissho Sushi has a flexible work schedule so it can provide quick-turnaround customer service to its partners as needed.

The keys of Maung's success are 1) having the right platform 2) focus on top customer service and 3) taking care of his own employees/associates. This creates consistent sustainability for Maung's business. So allow yourself to think big on developing the right platform to substantially increase the value of your business just like Maung's.

---

[21] Inghilleri, Leonardo. 2010. Exceptional service, exceptional profit: the secrets of building a five-star customer service organization. AMACOM.

INNOVATE OR BE CRUSHED

Innovate, Reinvent And Adapt For Ultimate Value Creation

Create growth opportunities beyond your current business model.

In nature, the plants that survive are the ones that can adapt quickly to changes in nature. Those that can't adapt quickly enough will vanish. The recent financial crisis has made businesses both large and small rethink their future direction. Even 100-year-old companies are learning to adapt and create ways to stay ahead of the game.

For small businesses, adaptation often translates into innovation. Innovation can be a product, process or service. It can be a business model, a new way of marketing, a new supply chain, etc. I had the opportunity to interview author Mark W. Johnson who wrote <u>Seizing The White Space: Business Model Innovation for Growth and Renewal</u>[22]. Johnson is co-founder and chairman of Innosight, a boutique consulting firm that helps clients improve their ability to create innovation-driven growth. Johnson says innovation can be part of your corporate culture—not a one-time deal—but a repeatable process. This repeatable process not only provides long-range strategic action for the business but also creates growth opportunities beyond the current business model.

For many small businesses, to be bought by bigger players could be a dream come true. But how do you position your business model so it is attractive enough to be bought? Yes, your product or service innovation has to be noticed. But you also need a solid foundation for the big guys to pick you up. Here are things to consider when you innovate or reinvent your business:

Focus on the job to be done. "A powerful customer value proposition is key to all successful business models," Johnson says. "The CVP can solve an important problem or satisfy a *job to be done*." Today, a B2C business can easily tap into the consumer's community and receive input from the community to enhance its products. "It is your job to fully understand your customers'/clients' *job to be done* so you can add value for all stakeholders."

The speed of new learning[23]. Any new business model needs timely implementation. "There are three stages in implementation:

---

[22] Johnson, Mark W. 2010.Seizing the White Space: Business Model Innovation for Growth and Renewal. Harvard Business Press. Boston.
[23] Ramo, Joshua Cooper. 2010.The age of the unthinkable : why the new world disorder constantly surprises us and what we can do about it. Back Bay Books.

incubation, acceleration and transition," Johnson says. Often, it takes years to go through these stages. However, the implementation stages are measured by the speed of new learning inside your business along with the structure, discipline and ability to trim waste in the system in pursuing potential growth.

<u>Scalability[24] of the new business model</u>. Whenever a business enters a new space, the owner is taking a certain amount of calculated risk. You have to know how to scale it so you can handle the growth.

<u>Financially fit to succeed</u>[25]. The five-year block (each five-year-block in a business is a milestone) often will determine whether a business can break through the $5 million, $10 million or even $50 million mark. To successfully apply the elements cited above, your business must be financially fit to take on the new challenge.

Parallel implementation. Don't rock the mother ship too much. Let the mother ship continue to sustain the business, and implement the new business model in parallel.

Remember this—your business either leads the industry or follows the industry. Where is your business?

---

[24] Colvin, Geoffrey. 2009. The upside of the downturn : ten management strategies to prevail in the recession and thrive in the aftermath. Portfolio.

[25] Wilkinghoff, Steve. 2009. Found Money: Simple Strategies for Uncovering the Hidden Profit and Cash Flow in Your Business. Wiley.

"WELL, LEARN TO RECOGNIZE MISSION CRITICAL ACTIVITIES"

Chapter 5

BVD Study Conclusion

My study has shown that the majority of business owners are in business because they want to make more money and gain financial independence. Over the years, I have observed many successful businesses and certain mission critical activities implemented by businesses. As a result, these business owners created value in their businesses and for themselves. However, not every business owner is equipped to recognize crucial mission critical activities.

I identified a total of 23 Mission Critical Activities (MCAs) for this study (found in the chart on Chapter 3), designed to reveal any participants who may already conduct these activities intuitively or without being instructed.

The reality is that most businesses are simply trying to make ends meet. Most will *not* be ten out of ten performers. Remember, according to the SBA, 95% of small businesses have less than $1 million in annual revenue. In every industry there are those who struggle, and there are always the exceptions that do extremely well.

So, what is the difference?

You see, for most business owners, no one actually taught them how to create, operate, and build a business—not to mention how to build value. The majority doesn't even know what *building value* really means. It has been my observation that those with immediate family members who grew up in the business learned subconsciously from their mother, father, or grandparents, who once owned and operated the business. These business owners tend to have a shorter learning curve, remain front-runners in their industry and demonstrate success very early on. As a matter of fact, 85% of the participants who indicated they grew up in a business environment worked for a family member at an early age.

But don't despair if that scenario does not describe your own business background. Incorporate Mission Critical Activities in your day-to-day operations, and over time, you'll see a real change in your business, your attitude as a business owner, and an uptick in your true business value.

Increase Ability.

Actions For Business Owners

The sixteen Mission Critical Activities (or 70% of total 23 MCAs; refer to the chart found on Chapter 3) used in my study indicated that more than 50% of participants need more training or information in order to be able to create value in their business.

On average, all 16 MCAs are important to business owners, yet the results indicate low to medium ability and that the tasks are somewhat challenging.

What does the study tell us about increasing ability?

- Everyone knows how to start a business, yet not everyone starts a business with an end in mind
- Intellectual properties have been overlooked and are limited to usage that simply generates more profits.
- The most important asset in a business is its people. But not everyone views people as an asset, therefore they fail to approach them as an asset, or most importantly, as an investable asset.
- Technology is moving fast, and is hard enough to keep up with, let alone leverage.
- To Increase ability, business owners or entrepreneurs must:
- Simplify business operations
- Seek resources for the MCAs
- Continue learning about MCAs and how to apply them in the business
- Work with a mentor or advisor to gain more insights about MCAs

Increase Challenge

Action for business owners

The twenty Mission Critical Activities (or 87% of total 23 MCAs) that indicated that more than 50% of participants need more challenge to enable them to create value in their business.

What does the study tell us about increasing challenge?

Everyone knows how to start a business, yet not everyone starts a business with an end in mind.

To increase challenge, business owners or entrepreneurs should:

- Redefine their mission and vision. Take the business to the next level.
- Increase standards, meaning raising the bar and measuring performance against higher standards.
- Change the task. Approach things differently such as creating a new customer base, packaging new products or services, or even considering a new geographic expansion.
- Reawaken emotions. When entrepreneurs first start their business, they usually have a clear mission/vision with compelling reasons. As the years go by and daily business operations become routine, there is no longer passion for that original mission or vision. They must re-ignite the fire they had when they began the business.
- Establish accountability. Business owners must simplify day-to-day activities and prioritize action items. Accountability must go beyond the checkbook or spouse. They must hold themselves accountable for increasing the value of their business.

Increase Drive

Action for business owners

The twenty three Mission Critical Activities (or 100% of total 23 MCA) that indicated more than 50% of participants need more drive in order for them to create value in their business.

To increase drive, business owners or entrepreneurs must:

- Revisit and realign passion. Drive is about passion. It is the internal force that moves us forward.
- Increase risks. There is no business growth unless the owner takes some risks.
- Identify the risk. Which risk presents the strongest likelihood of success and growth in both value and revenue?
- Stroking the ego. There are very few people who really know how to build up people.

Business owners feel pressure from many people depending on and counting on them. Owners must view themselves as leaders in their industry and present themselves in their company as a role model. To be a leader, one must take on a greater leadership role. A successful company can set the standard and be the benchmark with which to compare. Activity in industry associations, article contributions, etc. can move the owner toward being viewed as an industry expert. Working with a mentor, advisor or coach will benefit the drive of passion.

Appendix 1

BVD Study Results

Detail ChangeGrid® Data

About the Data:

This study focuses on the ChangeGrid® — a non-traditional coaching and management tool designed to explore individual and group performance and productivity through a highly client-driven, activity-specific approach.

Special thanks to Tension Management Institute for providing ChangeGrid® and its methods to facilitate this study.

Mission Critical Activities By Increase Ability

Mission Critical Activities	+ Ability
NJ_06: Transfer your business in the most tax efficient way	81%
NJ_04: Convert the value of your business into cash	80%
NJ_07: Maintaining healthy profit margin even if something were to happen to you or your business	75%
BVD_08: Determining the return on investment (ROI) of every productive employee	71%
BVD_13: Positioning processes to generate profit	70%
NJ_01: Determine the right market value of your business	68%
BVD_09: Evaluating ROI with each employee and team	67%
BVD_07: Leveraging marketing space for maximum sales	67%
NJ_08: Deploy measurable process to monitor business strategy	67%
BVD_12: Leveraging technologies to systematize processes	65%
BVD_05: Sustaining predictable revenue source	60%
NJ_02: Determine when to exit your business	58%
BVD_14: Implementing a set of Key Performance indicators (KPI)	57%

BVD_11: Streamlining processes with maximum efficiency	52%
NJ_05: Identify key value drivers for your business	52%
NJ_03: Replicate your current income for the next 20 to 30 years	52%
BVD_06: Sustaining Pull marketing (doors swings in your way)	50%
BVD_03: Diversifying revenue from products or services mix	46%
BVD_10: Developing synergy among key management team	43%
BVD_01: Earning profit on every client	42%
BVD_15: Maintaining healthy profit margin	42%
BVD_04: Diversifying client base	41%
BVD_02: Earning profit on every product or service	34%

Mission Critical Activities By Increase Challenge

Mission Critical Activities	+ Challenge
BVD_04:Diversifying client base	73%
BVD_03:Diversifying revenue from products or services mix	70%
BVD_09:Evaluating ROI with each employee and team	67%
BVD_06:Sustaining Pull marketing (doors swings in your way)	67%
BVD_11:Streamlining processes with maximum efficiency	67%
BVD_10:Developing synergy among key management team	66%
BVD_01:Earning profit on every client	65%
BVD_08:Determining the return on investment (ROI) of every productive employee	64%
BVD_02:Earning profit on every product or service	63%
NJ_05:Identify key value drivers for your business	62%
BVD_14:Implementing a set of Key Performance indicators (KPI)	61%

NJ_06: Transfer your business in the most tax efficient way	59%
BVD_13: Positioning processes to generate profit	59%
NJ_02: Determine when to exit your business	59%
BVD_05: Sustaining predictable revenue source	59%
BVD_15: Maintaining healthy profit margin	57%
BVD_07: Leveraging marketing space for maximum sales	56%
NJ_01: Determine the right market value of your business	55%
NJ_08: Deploy measurable process to monitor business strategy	55%
BVD_12: Leveraging technologies to systematize processes	54%
NJ_03: Replicate your current income for the next 20 to 30 years	49%
NJ_04: Convert the value of your business into cash	46%
NJ_07: Maintaining healthy profit margin even if something were to happen to you or your business	42%

Mission Critical Activities By Value Impact

Mission Critical Activities	+ Ability	Impact
NJ_06: Transfer your business in the most tax efficient way	81%	—Risks
NJ_04: Convert the value of your business into cash	80%	—Risks
NJ_07: Maintaining healthy profit margin even if something were to happen to you or your business	75%	—Risks
NJ_01: Determine the right market value of your business	68%	—Risks
NJ_02: Determine when to exit your business	58%	—Risks
NJ_05: Identify key value drivers for your business	52%	—Risks
NJ_03: Replicate your current income for the next 20 to 30 years	52%	—Risks
BVD_03: Diversifying revenue from products or services mix	46%	—Risks
BVD_10: Developing synergy among key management team	43%	—Risks
BVD_08: Determining the return on investment (ROI) of every productive employee	71%	+ EBITDA
BVD_13: Positioning processes to generate profit	70%	+ EBITDA

Work toward Reward

BVD_09: Evaluating ROI with each employee and team	67%	+ EBITDA
BVD_07: Leveraging marketing space for maximum sales	67%	+ EBITDA
NJ_08: Deploy measurable process to monitor business strategy	67%	+ EBITDA
BVD_12: Leveraging technologies to systematize processes	65%	+ EBITDA
BVD_05: Sustaining predictable revenue source	60%	+ EBITDA
BVD_14: Implementing a set of Key Performance indicators (KPI)	57%	+ EBITDA
BVD_11: Streamlining processes with maximum efficiency	52%	+ EBITDA
BVD_06: Sustaining Pull marketing (doors swings in your way)	50%	+ EBITDA
BVD_01: Earning profit on every client	42%	+ EBITDA
BVD_15: Maintaining healthy profit margin	42%	+ EBITDA
BVD_02: Earning profit on every product or service	34%	+ EBITDA
BVD_04: Diversifying client base	41%	+ High yield capital

Appendix 2

About The Study Participants

Since 2009, I have been conducting interviews and studies with business owners in the U.S. Notes and stories from the interviews have appeared in a number of my blog posts or even in this book. All interviews were used as a part of a study to identify statistical information on how business owners succeed in business. Approximately 14% of the interviewees' stories have been featured in my blog posts. Since my blog and my first book have thousands of readers, this provided a great opportunity to showcase successful businesses.

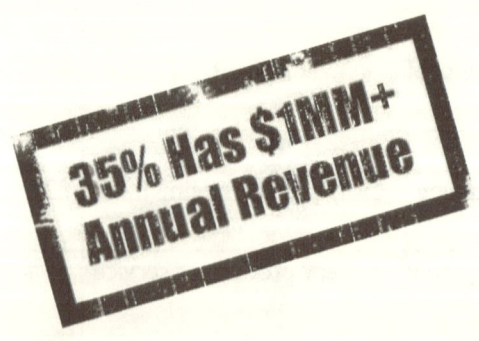

You can still participate! Don't miss this opportunity to have my subscribers and those who purchase my books find out more about your business both online and offline!

Where are my articles published?

- Chia-Li Chien's blog; http://chialichien.com/cal/blog.html
- Article Directory distribution from http://submityourarticle.com and top 10 article directories in the world
- Financial Planning Association – members only; http://connect.fpanet.org/home/
- Journal of Value Growth – members only; Value Growth Institute
- And many entrepreneurs' blog sites worldwide . . . and growing!
- Who are the BVD Study participants?
- Business owners who have owned and operated their business for more than 5 years
- Business owners who are the majority shareholder of the legal business entity
- Business with more than five employees and/or contractors
- Business owners whose businesses are not part of a multi-level marketing model
- Business owners whose business model is scalable and replicatable

Participants are asked to review the following to consider before the interview:

1. Review the sample Interview Release Form
2. Review Standard Interview Questions—pick 5 or 6 questions you would like to discuss

3. Complete an <u>on-line assessment</u>. It will take about 15 to 20 minutes

The time needed for the BVD study/interview

The majority of participants completed their assessment during the interview. The total time for the BVD study/interview takes about 50 to 60 minutes. It's optional for participants to schedule a separate date and time for reading of the business assessment. Participants receive three free downloadable chapters of my first book **Show Me the Money; Run Your Business Like a Prosperous Investor.** I notify the participants at a later date if the interview will be featured in one of my articles or my next book.

Most business owners have found the post-interview assessments insightful and informative, helping them to get or keep the business on track for success.

Nominate a business or participate in the study or nominate yourself! Would you like to let me know about customers, business colleagues or other businesses you are associated with or tell me about your own business? If chosen, a business could be featured in my blog just like the businesses you read about in this book. Check out the BVD study/interview at http://chialichien.com.

Appendix 3

Demographics of the participants

Key facts of participants:

- 93% of the participants are U.S. businesses
- 35% of the participants have more than $1MM annual revenue
- 86% of the participants have been in business more than 5 years
- 55% of the participants are women-owned businesses
- 7% of the participants are franchised businesses
- 81% of the participants started the business from scratch
- 28% of the participants have more than 10 employees
- 46% of the participants are S-Corporations
- 43% of the participants have more than one owner operating the business
- 38% of the participants have family members in the businesses
- 25% of the participants have a Buy/Sell Agreement in place
- 67% of the participants don't have a method to determine their own business value
- 54% of the participants consider their number one priority in business to be retaining clients

- 64% of the participants are over the age of 45
- 53% of the participants don't know when to retire
- 58% of the participants prefer to sell to third party when the time is right

Appendix 4

How The Study Is Conducted

All participants are asked to complete the two sets of assessments (http://chialichien.com) prior to a one-hour phone interview. Here are the two sets of assessments. Each assessment contains a number of the Mission Critical Activities that show what tension level is needed for them to build value within their business.

As a business owner, it would be a valuable exercise to complete an in-depth study of all Mission Critical Activities to ensure that you're creating value for your business. To get a feel for the assessment, rate the following mission critical activities value driver. Or go to our website http://chialichien.com for on-line assessment.

How to Complete Your Personal Assessment?

Remember that this is NOT a TEST. The value of your experience is COMPLETELY dependent on your willingness to be totally honest in your self-assessments. For each of the ACTIVITIES listed, you will be asked to rate yourself in three areas:

1. Rate your ABILITY to perform the ACTIVITY. ABILITY is made up of four elements: knowledge, skill, experience and physical resources. Ability ranges from a low of "0" to a high of "12". For each of the activities listed below, ask yourself, "On a scale of 0 to 12 — with "0" being "clueless" and "12" being "mastery" — how would I rate my ABILITY to perform this activity?" and write down your answer in the box located under the ABILITY row.

2. Rate the level of CHALLENGE or DIFFICULTY you feel the ACTIVITY represents for you. CHALLENGE also ranges from a low of "0" to a high of "12". CHALLENGE is made up of ABSTRACT variables, such as opinions, emotions, hunches, instinct and intuition. For each of the activities listed below, ask yourself, "On a scale of 0 to 12 — with "0" being "effortless" and "12" being "impossible" — how would I rate the CHALLENGE or DIFFICULTY of performing that activity?" and write down your answer in the box located under the CHALLENGE row.

3. Rate the level of IMPORTANCE the ACTIVITY holds for you. IMPORTANCE reflects priorities, preferences and deadlines and also ranges from a low of "0" to a high of "12". For each of the activities listed below, ask yourself, "On a scale of 0 to 12 — with "0" being "insignificant" and "12" being "critical" — how would I rate the IMPORTANCE of performing this activity?" and write down your answer in the box located under the IMPORTANCE row.

Business Value Drivers Mission Critical Activities assessment

BVD_01: Earning profits on every client
BVD_02: Earning profits on every product or service
BVD_03: Diversifying revenue from products or services mix
BVD_04: Diversifying client base
BVD_05: Sustaining predictable revenue source
BVD_06: Sustaining pull marketing (doors swings in your way)
BVD_07: Leveraging marketing space for maximum sales
BVD_08: Determining the return on investment (ROI) of every productive employee
BVD_09: Evaluating ROI on each employee and team
BVD_10: Developing synergy within key management team
BVD_11: Streamlining processes with maximum efficiency
BVD_12: Leveraging technologies to systematize processes
BVD_13: Positioning processes to generate profit
BVD_14: Implementing a set of Key Performance Indicators (KPI)
BVD_15: Maintaining healthy profit margins

Exit Planning (Next Journey™) Mission Critical Activities assessment

NJ_01: Determine the right market value of your business
NJ_02: Determine when to exit your business
NJ_03: Replicate your current income for the next 20 to 30 years
NJ_04: Convert the value of your business into cash
NJ_05: Identify key value drivers for your business
NJ_06: Transfer your business in the most tax efficient way
NJ_07: Maintain healthy profit margins even if something were to happen to you or your business
NJ_08: Deploy measurable process to monitor business strategy

Appendix 5

How The Interview Is Conducted

The one-hour agenda of the BVD study/interview includes these standard interview questions:

i. <u>Assessments</u>

    1. <u>Demographic data</u>

    2. <u>Mission Critical Activities assessments</u>

ii. Introduction

    1. Company product/services

    2. Company distribution channels

iii. Top 3 opportunities in your industry

iv. Top 3 problems or challenges in business, including financials.

    1. If you were to put a financial impact on these problems, what would that be?

2. What are the solutions?

v. 5 to 6 questions pre-selected by the interviewee

Participants are asked to choose 5 to 6 questions from these questions for the interview:

1. Why are you in business? (What's in it for you?)
2. What have you created from your business? (Job, lifestyle, 3x to 5x value?)
3. What is your passion?
4. What is your purpose? (Both in business and your personal life)
5. What are your core talents (competencies) used in your business? (Also including your personal talents)
6. How do you make money from your Passion/Purpose/Talents?
7. What gets you going in the morning?
8. What keeps you up at night?
9. What are the most common problems in your industry? (The industry that you serve)
10. What types of solutions do you provide or types of problems do you prevent?
11. How do you spot problems?
12. How do you learn? Not just to stay competitive, but ....
13. What is your marketing philosophy?
14. How do you deploy marketing systems to work toward your goals?
15. How do you check your business financial temperature?
16. Has there ever been a crisis in your life? What did you learn from it?
17. Do you upkeep your business? In ROI or value for you? (IP)
18. The U.S. has been the center of the universe (from most Americans' point of view) for the past 20 years. How

should we prepare for the future (both personally and professionally)?
19. How do you pay forward the success you have now? Or is that even an option?
20. Who has influenced you most in your business and personal life?
21. What's next for you?
22. What makes a business valuable?

Appendix 6

Transfer Methods

A. Internal Transfer

A-1. Employees

ESOP: Employee Stock Ownership Plans

In general, ESOP is a qualified plan (type of a company sponsored retirement plan) under ERISA (Employees Retirement Income Security Act of 1974). Employees enjoy the opportunity to participate and own a portion of the company via retirement plan contribution. From the owner's perspective, this will increase company cash flow because this type of contribution is tax deductible. It will potentially use the fair market value especially for those who may receive below fair market value when selling outright to a third party.

Businesses in the construction industry tend to use this transfer method, because the company typically only has equipment and contracts worth something to the buyer. Therefore ESOP is attractive to the construction industry as an alternative. It can also be designed to leverage ESOP in which the bank finances the deal instead of the owner. However, a company that has less than $2million[26] EBITDA is not a good fit. There is a complex setup; government regulation needs to comply with ERISA rules, annual report filing, and fees associated with this on an annual basis.

Management Buyouts or Buy-Ins (MBO or MBI)

When an existing key management team buys out the current owner you have MBO. MBI occurs when an outside experienced manager buys in from the current owner. The owner can engineer the deal to meet his or her needs by using tax-advantage structures, seller notes or earn-outs. Often this can be structured with leverage buyout such as banks, mezzanine capital and private equity groups. The deal will use the investment value instead of fair market value. The current owner needs to disengage over period of time to help to increase the value of the company. In addition to this structure, having a buy and sell agreement (see below for detail) and an employment agreement are great ways to address other risks or contingency.

Stock Appreciation Rights (SAR)

SAR is equity-based non-qualified deferred compensation that is subject to 409(A)32 unless using the fair market value of the underlying company stock as the initial value of the SAR. It is a corporate contractual promise to pay rather than an actual transfer of the company stocks. This typically is used as an incentive for a key management team to help a company reach a certain level of performance. If the expectation was met, then the company value goes up, the key employees get cash compensation instead of the company stock. This will not dilute the ownerships of the closely held business.

---

[26] Slee, Robert T. 2004. Private Capital Markets: Valuation, Capitalization, and Transfer of Private Business Interests. Wiley

Phantom Stock

This is very similar to SAR with the exception that it actually means underlying company stocks were set-aside for the key employees. That employee will receive the future benefits from the value of these stocks but not the actual stocks. This might be subject to 409(A); if not avoid "short-term deferral rule."

A-2. Charitable Trusts

Many business owners or entrepreneurs have charitable inclinations and desire to leave a legacy and enjoy the tax benefits. The tax benefits should not be the key driver for setting this up. In a nutshell, when you gift your company shares into a charitable trust, you are setting up an irrevocable trust.

Here are the benefits of a charitable trust:

The charity benefits from your donation. To receive your charitable tax deduction, the designated charity must receive the gift either before or after the term is up.

- Removal of capital gain tax—By doing so, the business owners will eliminate 15% to 20% capital gain tax in both federal and state taxes upon transfer into the trust. Most business owners start their business from nothing or next to it; therefore often experiencing a huge capital gain tax.
- Removes asset from estate; hence removing estate tax.
- Annuity of income for certain periods of time defined in the trust – you or your beneficiaries will enjoy a stream of annuity income either before or after a certain pre-defined number of years.
- Great tool to teach your family and build family legacy.

Charitable Remainder Trusts (CRT)

You enjoy the stream of annuity income from CRT, per the term (i.e. 10 or 20 years); the designated charity will receive the remainder balance of the trust.

Charitable Lead Trusts (CLT)

Charity receives the gift within the terms first, and then you or your beneficiaries receive the annuity income after the terms.

A-3. Family

Outright Gifts

There are two types of gifts that you can gift to anyone: One is an annual exclusion gift (at the time of the writing $13,000 per year per recipient). The second is the lifetime exemption gift of $1 million each donor. Both types of gifting require you file a gift tax return to indicate the transaction. For example, I can gift $13,000 to my daughter and my husband can gift her $13,000 without incurring any gift taxes (about 45% in 2009). Therefore per recipient, he or she can receive $26,000 per year without any gift taxes. Children who are in business with you can benefit from a transfer of company stocks up to this amount without incurring any gift taxes. The lifetime unified credit or lifetime exemption can only remove the future growth of the taxes. Upon death, it will come back to calculate into the estate taxes. Because of the complexity, please consult with your tax attorney before making final decisions.

Self-Canceling Installment Notes (SCIN)

This is a financing tool used to sell the business to family members. The note terminates upon certain events such as death. This note will not be included in the seller's estate if it contains an SCIN clause. Since it is similar to an installment note, it must have:

- Statement of the selling price based on appraised value.
- Statement of a fair market interest rate on the note – if not it will be treated as gift that is below the market rate.
- List of the terms of the note and payment amounts.
- Security interests in the business or some other assets.

This can also ease your capital gain tax burden since you are selling over a number of years. Each year when you receive the payment, you'll pay the portion that pertains to the capital gain tax. The seller's age is very important; otherwise the IRS will treat this as a gift.

Private Annuities

This is a financing tool used to sell the business to family members. It is an unsecured promise by the buyer to pay continued fixed payments for the life of the seller. This can be structured as single or joint life annuity.

Grantor Remainder Annuity Trusts (GRAT)

A structured annuity payment for a fixed time period. This type of irrevocable trust must use 120% of Applicable Federal Rate (AFR) as interest yield (published by IRS on monthly basis). This is an ideal estate planning technique if the company value is depressed due to the economic climate. (At the time of this writing, it is an opportune time to do so.) The assets in the GRAT ideally should outperform the AFR.

Family Limited Partnerships (FLP)

Essentially, the partners of this entity are all family members. Often time, the grantor or parent has many business entities and assets. For the purpose of centralized management, a family can structure this and allow the parents retain control over (as general partner) this entity while other family members simply enjoy the benefits of the entity distribution, if any. Upon the parent's death, the transfer will take place. You can take advantage of the minority discount upon transfer. The assets inside the FLP are protected from creditors. Since this is an area the IRS typically audits heavily, be sure to comply with all IRS rules.

Intentionally Defective Grantor Trusts (IDGT)

This type of irrevocable trust generally works well for a high growth company in which the company value is frozen at the time of the transfer. The company can pass on the growth from assets for a generation tax-free. This transfer is in exchange for a promissory note. Since there is no gain, or no loss, the sale is disregarded from income tax purposes. If properly structured, the future growth of company stock is tax-free for transfer purposes.

A-4. Co-Owners

Buy/Sell: Buy and Sell Agreement

A Buy/Sell agreement will address an orderly distribution of a business's shares in the event of the following triggers: death, divorce, personal bankruptcy, voluntary or involuntary terminations, loss of professional license, disability, and others. Within the agreement is indicated how the company value is to be determined and if there are financing terms from the company and what those terms are. Most entities have this section included in their operating agreement. However, it should be a separate agreement to address these trigger events, as well as the terms and conditions. In addition to addressing shares distribution, there should be a section about on-going management structure.

Russian Roulette

This buy/sell provision sometimes is referred to as mandatory buy/sell. The exiting party sets the price, and other owners buy the stock at the offering price. This provision gives the wealthier owner more leverage to control the process. Often this can be coupled with a promissory note.

Dutch Auction

In a Dutch auction, any owner can offer to buy another's shares. The responding owners could either accept or counteroffer the bid.

Right of First Refusal

The owner must offer to sell the shares to other owners before selling shares to outside parties. T Typically this is addressed in the agreement with a pre-determined price. From the outside parties' perspective, if they do not know the agreement has such provision, it might prolong the buying process or even kill the deal.

B. External Transfer

B-1. Outside (Retire)

Negotiated

In this highly customized, typically small deal in which the owner is the seller, market value is used. Ideally having an experienced industry transfer intermediary will help this process. There could be multiple buyers that are identified and negotiated with independently. The entire deal is kept confidential. The steps for negotiated transfer may include confidentiality agreement, information exchange, a letter of intent, buyer due diligence and closing.

One-Step Private Auctions

This type of auction has a limited group of buyers who are in the same industry as the seller. The seller believes there is only a handful of buyers in the industry that has synergy with their fi rm. The steps for one-step private auction may include: a confidentiality agreement, a selling memorandum, buyer visits, call for offers, negotiate synergy sharing, a letter of intent, buyer due diligence and closing.

Two-Step Private Auctions

This type of auction has a large group of interested buyers. The seller believes that they are highly desirable. The steps for a one-step private auction may include: a confidentiality agreement, a selling memorandum, buyer visits, call for offers, negotiate synergy sharing, a letter of intent, buyer due and closing.

B-2. Outside (Continued)

Consolidate

Driven primarily to consolidate the market space by buying more platform companies. The benefits of doing so, in addition to the market share, are cost cutting, revenue growth, centralized key management and benefits of size. There are three methods under consolidate; roll—up, buy and build, and recapitalization. Consolidation occurs in many Industries such as HVAC or staffing services.

Roll-ups

When consolidation combines with an initial public offering (IPO) it is called a roll-up. Sometimes it is referred to as "proof IPO" or "proof roll-up." It is a sell/trade, control-level, private equity for cash and a minority position for public entity. A roll-up is accomplished through the consolidation of many small businesses while simultaneously taken public. In the 1990s, there were many roll-ups and the performances of these companies often missed analyst expectations.

Buy and Build

This is a synergistic acquisition to build the company. This allows owners to continue to operate without equity risks. Either private equity group (PEG) or investment bankers guide the owners through 5 to 7 years of taking the company to the next level. Often the original owners may not have any equity position, but instead be in the key management team. There is deferred compensation to incentivize the management to grow the company in a pre-determined direction.

Re-Capitalizations

This is a process in which the owners sell part of the company to a private equity group (PEG) and continue to operate the company. In general, PEGs will own 80% of the company and consolidate with other companies they control. This is an ideal way for owners to cash in and combine with upside growth of the company. It's almost like selling your company twice.

B-3. Public

There are three ways private companies can go public:

- Direct Public Offerings (DPO)
- Initial Public Offering (IPO)
- Merging with existing public company or reverse merger

Direct Public Offerings (DPO)

This is a do-it-yourself initial public offering (IPO). The securities are publicly registered using simplified forms and procedures such as Small Corporate Offering Registration (SCOR) offering. SCOR is sometimes the early stage of venture financing using public investors as solicitations. The issuing company does not have to become a public company. The Pacific Stock Exchange will list SCOR securities.

Initial Public Offerings (IPO)

The first time the stock is offered to the public, that issuer becomes a public entity. The issuer registers with the Securities and Exchange Commission (SEC) and must file public disclosures. It must report quarterly to the SEC with Form 10-Q, submit audited financial statements on Form 10-K along with a periodic report of significant event on Form 8-K. A company worth less than $1 billion is better off remaining private.

Reverse Mergers

Private company mergers with existing public entities are called Reverse Mergers. It is the least expensive and quickest way to become public.

Going Private

A company is no longer required to file report to SEC. There is a high cost for compliance with the SEC.

Bibliography

- U.S. Small Business Administration Office of Advocacy FAQ http://web.sba.gov/faqs/faqIndexAll.cfm?areaid=24
- Mark Zuckerberg From Wikipedia, the free encyclopedia http://en.wikipedia.org/wiki/Mark_Zuckerberg
- Brown, John H. 2006. *How to Run Your Business so You Can Leave It in Style*. Business Enterprise Press. Golden, Colorado.
- Chien, Chia-Li. 2010. *Show Me The Money: Run Your Business like a Prosperous Investor*. iUniverse, Inc. New York.
- Slee, Robert T. 2009. *Midas Marketing, how Midas managers make markets*. Charlotte, NC: Burn the Boats Press
- Jackim, Richard E. and Christman, Peter G. 2006. *The $10 Trillion Opportunity: Designing Successful Exit Strategies for Middle Market Business Owners*, Second Edition. Chicago. The Exit Planning Institute.
- Slee, Robert T. 2004. *Private Capital Markets: Valuation, Capitalization, and Transfer of Private Business Interests*. Wiley
- Slee, Robert T. 2007. *Midas Managers, how every business they touch turns to gold*. Charlotte, NC: Burn the Boats Press.
- Slee, Robert T. 2010. Live Presentation: *How to Turn Your Business Into Gold?* Charlotte, NC. http://chialichien.com/cal/blog/309-how-to-turn-your-business-into-gold.html
- Covey, Stephen R. 2004. *The 7 Habits of Highly Effective People*. Revised edition . Free Press.

- Chien, Chia-Li. 2010. *What's Your $1 Million Business Worth?* http://chialichien.com/cal/resources/published-articles/125-whats-your-1-million-business-worth.html
- Kennedy, Dan S.; Jason Marrs (2011). *No B.S. Price Strategy: The Ultimate No Holds Barred Kick Butt Take No Prisoner Guide to Profits, Power, and Prosperity* . Entrepreneur Press.
- Kenneth H. Marks, Robert T. Slee, Christian W. Blees, Michael R. Nall. 2012. *Middle Market M & A: Handbook for Investment Banking and Business Consulting.* Wiley Finance. New Jersey.
- Johnson, Mark W. 2010. Seizing the *White Space: Business Model Innovation for Growth and Renewal.* Harvard Business Press. Boston.
- Gansky, Lisa. 2010. *The Mesh: Why the Future of Business is Sharing.* Portfolio.
- Pensak, David. 2008. *Innovation for underdogs: how to make the leap from what if to now what.* Career Press.
- Lewis, Michael. 2003. *Moneyball: The Art of Winning an Unfair Game.* W.W. Norton & Company.
- Mask, Clate. 2010. *Conquer the Chaos: How to Grow a Successful Small Business Without Going Crazy.* Wiley.
- Maney, Kevin. 2010. *Trade-off: why some things catch on, and others don't.* Crown Business.
- Huntsman, Jon M. 2008. *Winners Never Cheat: : Even in Difficult Times.* Pearson Prentice Hall.
- Lober, Rosalie. 2009. *Run Your Business Like a Fortune 100: 7 Principles for Boosting PROFITS.* Wiley.
- Bartiromo, Maria. 2010. *The 10 laws of enduring success.* Crown Business.
- Ramo, Joshua Cooper. 2010. *The age of the unthinkable : why the new world disorder constantly surprises us and what we can do about it.* Back Bay Books.
- Colvin, Geoffrey. 2009. *The upside of the downturn : ten management strategies to prevail in the recession and thrive in the aftermath.* Portfolio.

- Wilkinghoff, Steve. 2009. Found Money: Simple Strategies for Uncovering the Hidden Profit and Cash Flow in Your Business. Wiley.
- Warrillow, John. 2011. Built to Sell: Creating a Business That Can Thrive Without You. Portfolio.
- Inghilleri, Leonardo. 2010. Exceptional service, exceptional profit : the secrets of building a five-star customer service organization. AMACOM.

About Chia-Li Chien

Chia-Li Chien, CFP®, CRPC, PMP; Chia-Li "like JOLLY!" Succession Strategies for Women Entrepreneurs. Chief Strategist of Value Growth Institute, dedicated to helping private business owners increase the value of their firms. Award-winning author of **Show Me The Money** and faculty member of American Management Association. Chia-Li's blog and newsletter was named a Top Small Business Resource by the *New York Times* "You're the Boss" blog. To book Chia-Li for a workshop, keynote, or strategy session visit http://chialichien.com.

Chia-Li Chien, CFP®, CRPC, PMP
Succession Strategist
Value Growth Institute
13016 Eastfiled Road, Suite 286
Huntersville, NC 28078
http://chialichien.com
(704) 268-9378 jolly@chialichien.com

Nominate a business! Would you like to nominate customers, business colleagues or other businesses you are associated with? Or nominate yourself! Chosen businesses could be featured in my blog. Check out my annual BVD study/interview at http://chialichien.com.

Other Books by Chia-Li Chien

Show Me The Money: Run Your Business like a Prosperous Investor

Available at all booksellers Information at
http://chialichien.com

PROFITS MATTER® IGAP Workbook
Available only at Chia-Li Chien's Seminars, call for more detail.

Index

B

Business Architect 40, 43
Business Financial Behaviors 7, 8
Business model 20, 27, 28, 32, 33, 44, 45, 46, 61
Business Value Drivers xi, xii, xiii, xviii, 3, 7, 8, 9, 10, 11, 12, 13, 16, 27, 36, 47, 53, 54, 55, 56, 57, 58, 59, 61, 62, 67, 68, 86

C

Capitalizing 27
Customers 15, 18, 21, 27, 37, 41, 42, 43, 45, 62, 86

D

Decrease capital base 15

E

EBITDA 7, 8, 10, 11, 13, 58, 59, 72
Emotional Capital 17

Excellence 26
Exit Planning xviii, 81
Exit Strategy xv, 3, 27, 28, 29
Exit Triggers xvii
External Transfer 28, 29, 77

H

high-yield capital 7, 10, 15
Historic Business Value 10-Yr-Cycle 6

I

Impact Business Value 7, 10
Increase Ability 49, 54
Increase Challenge 50, 56
Increase Drive 51
Increase sales 11
innovation 41, 45
Intellectual Properties 21
Internal Transfer 28, 71
IPO xvi, 2, 78, 79, 80

K

KPI 9, 54, 56, 59

L

LEED 15
Leverage technology 35

M

M&A 22
Market Makers 27
Mission Critical Activities xi, 11, 13, 47, 51, 65
Mission statement 31, 32, 34

N

Niche 13

P

platform 17, 18, 19, 20, 21, 22, 23, 24, 41, 42, 43, 78

R

Reduce business risk 14
Reduce risk 7, 10
ROI 7, 8, 9, 11, 12, 13, 54, 56, 58, 59, 67, 69

S

Scale 20, 27
Succession Ratio xvi

T

Timing 5, 30
Transfer Methods xvi, 27, 28, 30

www.ingramcontent.com/pod-product-compliance
Lightning Source LLC
Chambersburg PA
CBHW030855180526
45163CB00004B/1583